DIFFICULTY

Also by William Logan

Sad-Faced Men (*David Godine*, 1982)

DIFFICULTY

POEMS BY

William Logan

DAVID R. GODINE
Publisher · Boston

First U.S. edition published in 1985 by
David R. Godine, Publisher, Inc.
306 Dartmouth Street
Boston, Massachusetts 02116

Copyright © 1984 by William Logan
First published in the U.K. by the Salamander Press

Library of Congress Cataloging in Publication Data
Logan, William, 1950–
Difficulty.
I. Title.
PS3562.0449D5 1985   811.54   85-70928
ISBN 0-87923-588-8
ISBN 0-87923-590-X (soft)

FIRST PRINTING
Printed in the United States of America

For my parents,
W. Donald Logan, Jr.,
and Nancy Damon Logan

Acknowledgments

These poems have appeared in the following periodicals:
Agni Review: Cartography; Florida; Hard Waters; The
Shootist. *Antaeus*: The Lost Fisherman. *Antioch Review*:
Money and Dürer. *Critical Quarterly*: Crows and DNA;
Flour Mites as Moral Beings; Stereopticon. *Epoch*: New
York. *Georgia Review*: Dream Contract. *Grand Street*:
Arcanum. *Iowa Review*: Questions of Waking. *Life*:
The Orchard. *The Nation*: From a Far Cry, a Return to
the City; Horace; The King of Black Pudding; Sutcliffe
and Whitby; Travel. *The New Yorker*: Jealousy; Winter
Garden. *North American Review*: Blue Yacht. *Sewanee
Review*: The Angels among the Liars; Folly; Green
Island; News of the Moon; Summer Island. *Shenandoah*:
The Country of the Imagination. *Southern Review*: Black
Harbor; This Island.

'Clare and Silence' appeared in *Journey from Essex:
Poems for John Clare* (Graywolf Press, 1981).

Many of these poems were written while the author
was an Amy Lowell Poetry Traveling Scholar.

Contents

The old conspiracy to make me happy! Everyone
seemed to be in it!

Bleak House

Clare and Silence

The grown faces men put on in their fits
are the fools of their imaginations.
The mad conscience this, the mad

delegate that, the mad live a mirror life,
hovering between the lark's
light exhaustion and the mortar of language.

We are the fashion of our dressy attitudes.
A man escapes from his asylum back into the world,
the world of waggons and dray horses,

of carrion birds and potters
burning in the fog of the marshes.
He escapes where the language no longer

incarcerates him in paper, where words
are only the wood, the church bell
tinning across cut fields. Such silences

are brief, a cold night in a hay cart,
before morning returns him to the prison
that exists and does not, that holds

and cannot keep, whose term is not
honorary or volunteer. Clare, your madness
confirms the losses that never were.

Arcanum

. . . as soon as I see the word arcanum *in any proposition I begin to suspect it.*

DESCARTES

Like Hegel's cows, chewing in the final dark
of reason, a domestic passion lies within
the *salus* of a language. Writing is a

privacy. I seal up that child of silence;
it turns its blank, dull face
to the world, and names a proper name.

On that adequate screen, the overcast sky,
what alphabets are traced? Scratchings
of trees, miserable spirals of chased birds,

homely parallels of planes. A writing
that seizes its own erasure, altering
the world it vanishes from. So the

homely alphabet: presence within distance,
ignorant messenger. Writing cannot
comprehend the lineaments of message.

Deaf to its own urgings, it outraces
presence, arriving before beginning,
always already the father of itself.

And the child of a silence, a feminine blank
that is famine and plenitude. Inscription
defaces the black monument of the word,

carving into an originary emptiness
an awful geography, after which all boundaries
are known, all geologies discovered,

all nature transcribed, though its
landmarks face outward, blind to the world.
The features name and are not named.

Stereopticon

How the flat century
bursts into illusionary depth, the ray
of marines drilling into
the distance of deck,
the sailor peeling potatoes under the

blurred eye of a hungry
goat, the meticulous barber shaving a
recruit as grinning sailors
look on. Colors whose
silence draws us in with lunar gravity,

into cool fixed diptychs,
stained-glass portraits whose interiors harbor
nothing but ritual pose,
bloom nevertheless
from sham separations into a writhing

mess of eels in a pail.
The divided eye wills parallax, honing
a weak horizon to sharp
discrimination,
entering a focused tableau, a frozen
land above the plates of

ice where naval splendor restores the drama
a photographer
takes in camera, giving
not so much the illusion of depth as the
reality of sight,

deluding itself with the double lenses
    that from the flat world
    steal a simultaneous
view, and from it brain that the world is not flat,
    but round, whole, dangerous

with depth. Our photographers abandon the
    will to educate,
    and our raw realities
turn silk-finished, heretical with color,
    flat and simple as steel.

The Angels among the Liars

Under trees where crows breed
despite what they have heard,
all nature observes the error

of the lying down of angels and men.
Even disreputable angels have a taste
for the human. Theirs is a mating

with the object of their disaffection,
for what impure angel otherwise
could power the air with longing?

What are the intermediacies of the body
but glazes, heavy and crazed?
And what is form but a contraption

of spirit? The forms asleep
beneath the withered fruit
are injunctions of a dusty surface.

Other men sleep well, knowing
there are no angels, and no words
that real or false will call them down.

Hard Waters

Much as the weary pump earns its water
from the forgiving earth, the dry harvesters
search among the trees for sweetness,

finding in a grove of almonds or peaches
a moment of intimate ripeness. Where swollen
clouds blur the western sky, a latitude

suffers against this astringency of weather.
Hard water interrupts the weakening skin,
lives are quenched by drowning. The red trains

steam back and forth along the valley tracks,
attached here to uneasy waking, a dream
that draws nothing from ripeness. Unwanted fruit,

bagged and dropped into the river, rots downstream
on the gravel washes. Nothing completely
earns its way: the old orchard will be cords

of hardwood when the men have done
their work and the rains have come, whiplashing
the yellow lawns. Ashes by spring.

The lessoned hours count imperfect fruit
that make a harvest. Half for storage, half waste,
a payment for what lasts through winter.

Who could tire of the false variations of sky
when any night can level the corn
or take from the trees an unripe fruit?

The modifications of our calm are harsh, the cost
of watching lizards hurtle through the garden
on the measured path of the sun. Winter rains

have laced the valley and the morning dust
chills a whitish garden. Men measure themselves
for their beds. There is no flat comfort

when what is gone cannot reprove us:
in this land or any other there comes
a reminiscent weather, menacing the kindness

we hold for ourselves. Winter memory
is a guilty return to what error and love
have built. In late afternoon, the day

seems unnecessary and small, too apparently
lost in sepia. Among survivors,
there is a method: prime ministers and generals

die first, then colonels, leaving
a century after only an ancient private
who to be able to enlist lied about his age.

III

Slow light wastes the colors of the ridge
where fire finds no hold. When the seed grass
blows indifferently, the rains ruin months

of farming, and drive the hiker upland
to observe the light sliding off toward the sea.
The solvent species exist under the gaze

of a blank eye. How long until the blindness
is washed clear, until the fields below, rice
and safflower and corn, resume their individual

focus? Beneath the raw grass, never rising for air,
there is a manner that cannot be immanent.
It is unwilled and uncontrollable. A farmer

strikes off for the fields through dead summer,
knowing that two days of hard water
will swallow him. The irrigation ditches

cut steadily through the fields with a low glamour,
yet in the hills dry holes chase declining water,
and shafts sink toward bedrock.

Much remains irrecoverable after a day waiting
for the rain's exhaustion. Such residue returns
the hiker to hills that have nothing else to offer.

The Orchard

The evening light slaps the orchard floor
where twisting sprinklers hurl their load
through gnarled lines of peaches.
Summer cannot equal

the weight of the poisonous Caesars.
A mottled snake insinuates the field,
its corded body bulging to disclose
the gopher's swallowed form. It is not

poison or a look that hyponotizes, but
the sudden shocked surrender men
have reported when mauled by a bear.
Still, when high on pride or mutual fear

a squad of soldiers moves into a minefield,
knowing the distances they keep
are to limit their mistakes,
their acceptance of a necessary duty

reminds them of the odds of death,
where every soldier's equal fear
will average the iniquity of war
if war is long and death almost sure.

When Varus and his legions vanished on the Rhine,
fruit brightened in Rome's orchard
and the Tiber's grove. Though Rain Birds
and drip pipe have overthrown the aqueduct,

modern irrigation differs little.
The cultivated peach swells faster than the wild.
Its ranks are spaced no wider
when the soldier is at war.

News of the Moon

The desk lamp, an incandescent moon,
hangs over the hard plain of the desk.
Lesser astronauts leap for the light.

Their bodies curl beneath its radiance.
I am naked against these breaches
of possession. Your sickness exchanges

the sky for a rotting onion,
shedding rings upon the bruised air
until a last scorched light steadies

the horizon and stars burn in.
How calm and convenient the night,
its hunter, fixed animals, and sturdy wagon,

a dumb show beyond the pines.
Grasshoppers perched in the plum
savor its indigo leaves.

Mackerel clouds swim upside-down
in the river above, and fishermen
cast for air. The house is a pump

and all the outer animation floods
the starved chair and cracked bed.
The body's intimate routine

thrills to its premature rot, its cellular
drama. Reduced to the scope
of the fossil, each mineral grain

seeking hermitage in the cell,
the night's granular sky
is more and more possessed

by an architecture not its own.
Each sunset seems an electric hesitation.
Each sunrise burns like a ghost.

Jealousy

Philosophers rise at 3 a.m. to undercut
the advantage of dawn. In the yellow houses,

ideas knock shyly at the French doors.
Mornings unwind in a month of exhaustion,

the car stalling at intersections,
the gophers undermining the yard.

A silent caller knows the number of our telephone,
and I invent for you a book of lovers,

each with his appointment and halting speech,
a dream life become life, a method of distance

come home. But the streets are plains,
not planets. The bearded professor stares

at my hands, his interest anatomy,
not passion. Jealousy is the art of behavior,

the visualized future again and again
held to the blind present, as the flicker

flees the woodshed at our soft approach,
until the morning it is gone, a second winter

traversed in pine and insulation. Like your phantom
lovers, seasons to pass through. The full moon

ignites a common scene, the ideas frozen,
the barn bleached of color,

the hole in the shattered window
an emptiness the shape of Australia.

Money and Dürer

Our heedless statesmen here lose their heads
and from their silent mouths
admissions flourish, trusting in such a one,
taking *e pluribus* such another:

How unprepared, the rich,
like the gray knight in 'Ritter, Tod, und Teufel,'
facing obstacles other
than his handbook described, expecting
the press of metal
on his back and belly, the spear clothed in fur,
to intimidate the Devil and Death:
Ignoring them, he hopes to find some small
valley where dragons are mortal,
spear aslant shoulder, far from the walls
buckling their cables:
He finds long days where a hostage sun hauls color
from the barns of the dead:
The shattered stalls, the stringy cows
seem too earthly symbols
of heavenly complacency: His warhorse nibbles
hay at his feet:
He dreams valleys where the dead die, and work off
the debt of dying,
always with other, poorer valleys to slave in,
deeper into the famished
alleys of death: He wakes to empty plains:

The stars are needles, the fields full with grain:
Meteors prick the seamless sky:
Now bare lanterns light the lurcher home,
where money
sleeps outside the houses of the poor,
cool unreasonable planets
turning one face to the viewer, like love.

Black Harbor

Love denies the precincts of its will.
Though August's busy windstorm swarms
the air of sheltered harbors, brooding harm
against the anchors of the day,
there is no number inked against the kill
that rusts the standing grain. A small hawk swerves
to claw the sparrow its alchemy deserves
and burning windows light the gravel way.
Through season, season, while miners hammer
needles into veins of cannel coal,
the rabbit crawls exhausted to its hole
and dying bees lie mired in the comb.
The crippled hand derides the fetid summer.
The grass absorbs philosophies of bone.

Summer Island

We leave the farmland for the formless coast
where broken wreaths of breakers trouble
the luckless gull. Past the driftwood litter,
seals loll and bathers sag toward water.

Our landlocked cottage lifts its eaves
above the brassy bay. To and from
the dumpy port, a shuttling mailship
cheats the tides. The damaged lighthouse winks

and aims its eye over the rolling horizon,
where time shuffles its hour
and land settles seaward.
Odd seasons the locked plates shake

the bearings of the hills and grease
the granite monuments. We cannot wait
for nature's declaration of the breach
that bonds the island to the land. A scarred

seawall carves the current back to shore.
Light swings crazily on the corrugated wake.
Back and forth the peeling buoys twist
like targets. Tomorrow we will separate.

Questions of Waking

I wake, having dreamt again of a conclave
sessioned in a narrow room
while a moon like a narrow heart faltered

to the horizon. What hold has death
over this easy breathing? An empty cry sounds
from the orchard, a labored inhalation as if

something were whining for air. That is the burden
of dreams. Every morning an animal lies
battered on the road—opossum, squirrel, raccoon.

Their bodies annoy, as do the dogs howling
at the pitch of the sirens, some atavistic chorus
aroused by a voiceless stirring. There is

no escape here from the feelings of animals.
After sleep has been used to avoid
an hour alone, who can help feeling diminished?

I wake among walls as null as dreams,
but until the moment of recognition arrives,
I am satisfied with the dull procession

of imagination, as if that accomplished all
that needed to be done. Then the cars grind by,
their faulty mufflers booming,

and the rooster empties his voice
into the surrounding yards. What use
to struggle against a meeting of possibility

and death? The harvest moon,
swollen and globular, has spent its orange light.
It must return in a different year.

Crows and DNA

This rootless blue light, heir to storm,
hangs over the yard like passion

deified. Or desperate. How sudden crows
black the air suits a languorous discussion,

not this awe of natural signs.
Heaving up the slow encumbering shore,

Atlantic waterspouts retain a light
beneath the skin.

Volcanos impose their immediate weather.
This rational landscape suffers

no shudder in the grass, no abrupt
and temporary seizure except angled crows.

They converge on the maples and cry.
They wheel over the streets and return

like widowed, irritable pilgrims.
What turns their precedents? The imperial

love of oracular moment. A single twining thing
replicated and joined. These

feathered particulars are the shadows of form;
yet once, in false fog,

above a chasm in Pennsylvania,
a lone crow perched on the bridge rail,

opening its wings to the weather,
the sole observer and inhabitant.

Dream Contract

Storms blow, termites gnaw wood,
but the principles of this contract
are founded in rock, the principles
of this contract have been entombed,
the principles can neither be bent
like reeds nor stayed like horses.

The rights retained under this contract
rise above it like a faculty, the rights
are a taproot. Your rights depend
like cut glass from a chandelier,
like bare leaves from the oak branch.

The rights of this contract are adamant;
they can neither be conquered by armies,
sedimented by rivers, nor bridged by engineers.
They cannot be undermined by sappers
or surprised by assassins. They cannot be
seduced, danced upon, or devoured;
they are the unusable dowry,
the unbreachable trust.

The parties to this contract are united;
with age their union will not discolor
or flow like glass, will not trade season,
will not decay. The fetters of this contract
are incorruptible. The ropes have been tied
with fine knots.

Shores melt away, bridges collapse,
rivers change course, country eats country,
but the principles of this contract

are steadier than the pole star, the rights
of this contract more stable than earth,
and the parties to this contract yoked
more steadfastly than Earth to Moon.

The Lost Fisherman

Tides wallow in the inner valley
no more than the degree of rain or moon
that stiffens the river with a nominal
surge. Trees flattened on its surface
stray no further than the ringlike shimmer,
where swelling bullheads nip images
when mouthing flies, but watch for lines
and dodge the plastic worm. How like
a snake clear-bellied water lies,
and in the snake the starving salmon
buck the flow and fin upstream until
their meat dissolves in natal pools.
There I argued the malarial fog away
and found the moon's full disk and its wafer
on the surface waver toward each other,
and the cylinder of light that joins them
anchor the river to the air.

I fumbled through thick weeds like a turtle.
Sunk into the bank against the losses
of erosion, the shells of cars repair
with mud. What violence does delta
call for? Where the bay generates its backwash
and a scroll of waves unmakes the flat
illusion, three men have spun a week
beneath the current until spurned
upon the gravel beach. From floodplain and eddy
past drift and drywash, toward a cottonwood
grove islanded by this year's course
and last year's bed, the inlanders came down
with flashlights and dogs, and girdled
the outer stand for the fishermen's fire.
Down to the river the charred fields stretch,

where they have found an ancient anger in dry grass
and winter fills the shallow bay with dead.

A foreign nature marks a foreign nature
strictly. Upstream spring hauls its load
of lumber from the hills. Pitching through
the muddy channel, the sharp limbs ride
above the swell like masts. Beavers clamber
up the banks, their creek-dams shredded
and unwoven, nestling in split vines
until the fresh bark scarcens. Nothing
walks the muddy roil but the skinny heron,
piercing blank water for blind food.
Filling the belly of the riverbed, rain
shoulders rock downstream another yard,
undercuts the mansion and the pier.
I watch the falling Dipper dump the flood
that sculpts the canyon lava into
birdless cavities, where native blindness
sees a raw world in a foreign soil's loss.

Cartography

As children you and I mastered maps,
passionate for Siam and the Gold Coast,
wary of Father, rattled by burnt toast
or anything capricious, unsure, perhaps

mutable. So every day, the view
from his office turning cuprous at sunset,
he lowered his blinds, as if to forget
the inconstancy cities were subject to.

At sixty Father vanished in Japan
and left you the inheritance of work:
the devious janitor, the brutal clerk,
the elevator run by a crippled man.

Your bay windows face—what else?—a bay
on which, deserted, a prison island sits
in tropic splendor. The tourist board permits
tours that ferry over water one day

blue as a blazer, the next like sour milk.
That island is as near as we have come
to jungle, where poppies bleed pure opium
and garden caterpillars excrete silk.

Our father on a foreign pier grows old.
Our adolescent wishes now dismay us.
Our parents in the end betray us
for wanting other lives than they controlled.

The Country of the Imagination

The black dogs come down from the passes
where mendicants eat flies off the faces
of the dead. It is not a religious spring,

even in the country of the imagination.
In the meanest world,
the success of adjacent mornings

is measured by a swollen light
unmarked by death. A red sun succeeds
the uneven rim of atmosphere. By noon

willows stand dying along the concrete
irrigation ditch, once a rough creek.
The leaves rattle their silvery, mothlike

undersides. The real religious find
their followers speaking stringent languages,
whose vocabulary cannot guess

the intention of the straw-haired woman
sweeping a frieze
of grasshoppers from her porch, or the

awkward dead in the dry grass, or the men
burning the nesting field. Language
banishes the behavior of its times.

Evenings, across acres of plowed field,
a scruffy peacock cries. Leashed to a
splintered stake, it squawks demands

within a reduced geometry, and pecks
a stony meal under transplanted bamboo.
In the imagination it no longer exists.

Winter Garden

The pump, on and off through evening,
works to raise a winter garden, now that
tomato leaves hang sour and lifeless

on the chain-link fence, and the three-branched
squash plant decorates the mulch pile.
Through summer, though almost in another country,

barn swallows gleaned young mosquitoes rising
off a lake, never falling through its calm mirror;
yet today a California jay dove against

the picture window, breaking its intemperate body.
What drove it against that attacking reflection,
to die incongruous under the ornamental roses?

If on the other side of all water lies death,
nothing keeps us from reaching toward it,
toward that full, alternate land lying beyond

a sequence of trains stumbling along the river,
where nothing is reflected but trees precarious
on the flood plain, or the careful herons

patrolling their banks. In another world,
fish view a watery sky, unaware of the beak
that may pluck them into air. Subdued

by the waters we lie in, we cannot see what sweeps
frost from the valley, or casts down the mastering snow.
We cannot mistake yellow light refusing

the afternoon orchard or know when,
so illumined, a bird glides toward a cold window
and flies out blazing in an alien air.

From a Far Cry, a Return to the City

Again its familiar skyline swims
into the blanketed vision of the traveler
who after miles of snow, the rear of farms,
the rusting bridges of an iron technology,

welcomes architecture challenging
from the scale of the long-distance train.
The template of its horizon suggests
a lost branch of physical taxonomy

where patterns of height fix character,
as surgeons once diagnosed illness
from the lumps of the head. Entering
its arterials, like a bacterium, one

loses the outward view, discovering
a gaudy language in the graffiti
of the dispossessed. But even here, having
lost through absence the anger of caution,

one for a time enjoys the passport
of the immigrant, one's future tongue
awkward and strained, and sees from within
its resemblance to the body of other capitals:

subject to scales of diminishment, unused
to hours or calendar, populous with
forlorn generals horseback in traffic circles.
Whether center of a temperate duchy

or a dictator's tropical madness, each
individuates the argument of its own case,
though alike as any terminal where the tired
can store their luggage and find a telephone.

New York

At dawn the cornering taxis cast
headlights through your darkened room
like a junkie's flashlight fingering
the walls, finding no stereo, no jewelry,

just the cool uncaring plaster.
The wrinkled super wrestles garbage cans
to the curb, their dented lids
at a rakish slant. From the third floor

schoolchildren, no angels, descend
in shouts. They might be angels of a low
order, given to almost human display.
On your windowsill, a stagnant pond

fills from its secret spring: the upstairs
neighbors' leaky radiator. Yesterday the super
muttered that there were no upstairs
neighbors. Can he be hiding relatives?

When you return, the street is already
silent, though on the avenue grunting semis
crawl. You cross beneath a leafless tree
the streetlight settles a nimbus on,

and pass a spray-painted wall:
MAMBO JANE WANT TO DRESS YOUR GIRLFRIEND.
A man in an expensive suit makes a rubbing
of a manhole cover. The brass mailbox

is full of foreign mail. In the sliver of sky,
a malignant moon skulks above the brownstones,
now wrapped in cloud, now confused
in a welter of antennae.

Florida

a postcard

The parrots are nailed to their perches—
I can tell from their depressed gaze,
martyrs staring with avian blankness
at a heaven of oranges they assume are eggs.
No earthly fruit swells to such proportion
unless cultivated somewhere near Mars,
but below them a priestly alligator rears its head
in a gelatin pond. Its mouth propped open,
it has held this yawn since Audubon's arrival
with only a motley sunrise to contemplate.
Or sunset? Is the Atlantic or Gulf sky
painted these liturgical purples,
a backdrop that wouldn't fool a child
or the imaginary friend of a child?

How respond to your Technicolor horizon
except to note imbibition has been abandoned,
no longer cost efficient? Old movies—shown now
in old moviehouses subdivided like old estates—
even in your country fade to the color of old blood.
Quartered like a coat of arms, your card
heralds a daughter whose families surely
took arms when the Caribbean was plundered,
finding in names (Orange, Parrot) a tropical genealogy,
leaving ancestry mixed and mired here:
three stunted palms, sable, line the needle beach,
hardly inviting habitation. There is none.
Across the sky, bend sinister, in neon calligraphy,
Florida. The schoolmaster's favorite peninsula.

Blue Yacht

No opening line ruptures the surface
of silence better than any other.
Already the work has been accomplished
by the brave title. Farewell, title,

now receding into the impoverished memory.
Interjections and farewells
accomplish little toward sinking a well
through the thick, impermeable rock face

of silence toward—toward what? Not memory
or passion. Or possession. Toward another,
less agreeable silence, the underside of title,
the dolmen marking the limit of accomplishment,

beyond which is *terra incognita*. Accomplishment
for its own sake is odious. The well
or sane do it for money or title,
the nobility or wealth beneath the surface

of feeling. One man is never as good as another.
None of us will last long in memory.
Similarly, no line lasts long. Like emory
board, the abrasive accomplishment

soon effaces the rightful claims of other,
older events. More aggressive lines soon dwell
vividly on the capricious surface
of memory. Take our forgotten title,

doddering into the past like Lear. Similar titles,
other bad beginnings confuse the memory
until that title, that small ship at the surface,
is as forgotten as air to the accomplished

diver. Here the weight of lines swells
the brain as it compresses the body. Other
lines, constantly piling up, smother
the raptured memory. What was the title?

Not even the darting fish remember it well.
What was projected as a silly exercise in memory
is now a *fait accompli*.
We have ended what began at the surface.

Difficulty

I

An evening. Each sunset window finds its flame
arising in the glass, a phoenix woken
to the mirror of lime, soda, silicate
spread to receive winter's blushing detail—
the rose unpetalled, the chalky slush, the peeled
Vermeer of a painted wall. The glassy fire
burns like fever. The scene, ablaze, goes dark.

You cannot help the absence or the want.
Ten years have passed. Those years have built
windows through the painted scenes, landscape
frozen into fashion. But still cold sunlight
will call a moment back from darkness: two lovers
in a snowy field, days before spring broke
violently upon us. The snow was fresh.
We found the bloody tracks a bird had left,
crossing from scrap pines to thicket. We followed
the halting tracks deep into the woods,
driving it before us. We didn't know.
A ragged clearing spread the sun around us.
Beneath a tree, its chest a wound, the grouse
cast a bloody shadow on the snow.

The world grows disenchanted with birds, not birds
crying hunter from nest and egg, but the small
anatomies of sparrow, starling, crow,
the common fowl of laundry and backyards,
the days that pass to night in plain array,
distinguished neither in pain, love, rage.
There is fire in the world that is not all
passion. Burning coldly, it burns without you.

Love's the boy stood on the burning deck—E. BISHOP

How take a root from the radical of passion?
These houseplant days, a simple graft will fail
the mandate of its kind. And kin to no one,

the solitary spy finds his ancestry
dissolved in granite monuments and tombs,
a splay of ivy giving green light to stone.

Call the spy love. Give him the enigma
of his calling, the shadow on the border
of the old autocracies. A year

yields its single secret, coded over
and over until its message erodes. Love
is that erasure, that small error repeated

until the margin is large, a rocky shore
the cold sea drags its weight against. The sea
derives its own mathematics, sequences

of storm and wreck, the vertebrae of dunes
answering their seasonal commands.
The sums of plants and animals divide

between themselves the world of loss and weight,
and in the files of that world old passions
gnaw, silent for years and then, gorged on pain,

monsters again. Passion's the bureaucrat
who set these acid pages face to face.
Passion's the mutant plant, the gutted fish,

the ship afire. Passion's the dead spy.

In one or two cities I imagined you had passed
days, hours, minutes ahead: the last
train blurred into smoke, the stations played
anthems to platforms of the damned and delayed.
Verdammte Traume. Were dreams maps: progression
of the hours, Mercator's grid, compass rose,
mechanical contrivance meant to show
the dark that weighs the light weighs the dark?

No winter orchestra could celebrate
Mozart's birthday in the January
thaw—the dandy, dead at thirty-five,
whose black and white keys sickened speech and nights.
You danced among the notes, a European temper
that endows economies in sorrow,
zones in pain, the puzzled countries
a fevered hand devours. The cardboard globe's
a toy, but on it rest olive valleys
the heavy rivers drain, pale yellow deserts,
seams that piece country to country's doubt.
Anger's a music until it wears play out,
its needle skipping through worn passages,
its globe awhirl on a metal rod.

IV

She's not alive. It's this I must remember.
The low islands shudder in sea light.
How many geometries of art have we

endured? She stands within the cottage room,
image and reflection of us both.
We can't survive the art we artlessly

engender, shameless politics of feature
Elizabethan in their metaphor—
her smoky pear skin, eyes brown as winter caves,

that lion grin, the still blue veins aslant
her jaw. The mirrored room's a nature where
we have a phantom daughter, hollowed out

of marble confidence whose years have nothing
to say to us; reckless and burdened, they
reconcile nothing to nothing. I can't admit

absence draws its life out of flesh. She's only
a circumstance of self that nothing reconciles.
Each session at the mirror I should know

that art is not truth. Art has no face.

v

In silhouette, a man wrestled with his daughter.
Along the black ice of the hill
she slid past him, wobbled, faked a spill.
They broke into a thorny laughter.
I envied them their flashing moment
plucked from the lakeside fragments

one year's leisure deposits for the next.
Your photographs, frozen like still water,
have no mark of spring, the cruel otter.
Design without speech, face starved of text,
it does not promise what it cannot deliver.
I burned our letters that winter,

clumsy dissections of passion's reach.
Your once familiar blue
scrawl became a scroll of ash, more true
where pictures alone are honest teachers.
From a sputtering match at the corner of the sheaf
the flame coiled upward, leaf by leaf,

into a hideous flapping seraph,
grinning icon of the lost.
We learned what rough accounting costs,
the honing of the laugh
for students who, their musculature from books,
approach where naked men and women sway on hooks.

VI

The bank was steep, shaded with burning palms,
the oasis small, and littered with turtles.
Who knows how they were brought
into that unhappy desert? It had been a long,
fruitless journey, and we were eager
to return, loaded with knives
and gifts for our daughters.
The pool glowed with dust, and the horses,
impatient of water, twisted their necks
and pawed the sand. We reined them back.

Over the bank a vulture glared,
its eyes the only red in that pale land.
Around its feet a papery eel had coiled
its gluttonous body.
The waist-thick palms shuddered,
their scaly trunks swaying like cobras.
In the stillness, broken only by the snorts
of our horses, the shuffle of fronds, the deaths
seemed a greater stillness.

The red eyes moved, the mummied eel shifted.
We poured the dirty water over them,
then drew the eel into a broken barrel
and waded it out upon the pool.

We had come many miles to so small a shore.
It may have been dream. It seemed a dream.
We had seen many perverse couplings and had come
out of that land with a manifest of evil.
We let the horses drink. The vulture crawled away.

VII

How give these human lineaments
a bearable name? Unanchored by time,
disease, or the small refunds of love,

the face drifts into squalls of memory
when posture or the particulars
of reflection harbor in forgetfulness.

Except when the stranger is the self,
most are prisoners to another's body.
Visible in the angle of cool light,

the almond eyes stare out from the prison
of the lover's flesh, toward the lack-shine
prison here endured. The mask frightens

not by resemblance to the dead
but in mimicry of the living: who has not
found among the animate the inanimacy

of passion, emotion still and violent
on a surface tender in decay?
To take these lines lies master,

the apportionate geometry feature follows,
is to accept a darker window,
the four panes behind which rises

the distant planet of the face,
glassed off from guilts
it is necessary to repeat and repeat,

subject of a painter who for difficulty
applies to every diverse profile
the identical involute ear.

VIII

The bustling radiator, the broken clock
whose frozen semaphore regards the hours
with a mute disdain, the faucet dripping
iron tears into its iron sink—
how violent the world they dispossess.
You sat one night, the marble ashtray wedged
with cigarettes your narrow lips had stained,
a hand beneath your chin, watching movement
swell the carpet, one oriental sea
bleed slowly into another, the stable shores
collapse before the skittish waves, to drown
and be renewed in battle on opposite
quarters, opponents in a conflict
no god controlled. Or general contained.

I see, again, you as you must have been
ten years ago, waiting for my call.
Your blond hair brighter then, darker now.
The vein within your forehead, a narrow seam
drifting toward your right eye while a blue
nerve pulsed beneath your left. You said

each night words you never wanted to say,
words you never meant. Each night I called
to hear them said again. You never meant them.
Each word an acid lake, in which dead fish
night by night surface, chalk-white bellies
to the moon while, beneath them, scavengers grow
more vicious, feeding on their offspring, feeding
on themselves. Lake of Deception. Lake
of Dreams. Lake of Loss. You never meant them.
I understand that now. I understand the love
that twists us into lives we never meant.

One long night, before you were pregnant,
you held a wet cloth to my head and hour
after hour whispered love into my ear.
I know better what those whispers meant.
Or tell myself I know. The clock has stopped,
whose hour comes by accident. The carpet's
in the attic. You're never coming back.

Sutcliffe and Whitby

The sea, that problem Euclid never solved,
whose black rooks curve
linear demeanors of the shore, burns

under the abbey, a little selfishness
made grace. Neither we, nor the stable-yards,
nor the knacker's tumbled house,

the dead harpooner's cottage, color
the lobster-claw piers pinching
this resort's slummy river from sea,

where the whale's cheesy body wept into wicks,
and jet was ground into tokens
for the living for the dead, a grief of soft coal.

Singers in the sea-wracked graveyard
make early music an English
proposition. Down from the heather

where sheep gather by milestones,
the rude parishioners clatter floors
their fathers' fathers' fathers laid.

We are only the false-coated crew,
the humbled watchers stirring at shipwreck,
while men in open boats oar out and back.

What mastery lies in leaving?
From history fails one landscape, not
the sea exposing its fragile negatives.

Travel

Sir, to find an answer
is not easy among the nervous mass.
Draw near the exile, note his fingers

manicured in pavilions, and the feet
in soft shoes shod. Often from lands
he departs in vanity's offices, knowing

the luxury of refusal; yet how easy
to mistake for courage is fear's glance.
The milk-brick walls

call the hotel creatures into form—
the hourly animals, awake at nine,
brunching at pond-side tables on carp:

a vested hippo, an Anglican giraffe,
the neurasthenic elk beneath their veils.
They too recede, with their daring clothes

and ridiculous manners, footnotes
to footnotes in the loose masonry
of scholarship. Where even accidental poise

receives the imprimatur of history's architect,
who sees beyond careless wanderings
the emotional clatterings of the age?

Fashion alters politics or love:
like sexual anxiety, what is lost
is not so much abandoned as converted

at the Bureau de Change, one currency
for another, tawdry bills commemorating
a presidential fool or dowdy queen.

Horace

The master plies the instinct of the slave
with jewelry heavy on his gristly wrists,
a drowse of circumstance within his eyes
like vapor of an overturned perfume.

And still the varying light remembers there
uncertainty on marble, the dictator
wheezing where, bleeding now of larks,
refrigerated dawns, he saw harsh pines

lean back toward sea and a mortgaged farm
open shallow fields to grain and reason.
The palace injunction like a cord extends
over local cobblestones and walls,

exhausted shields, nets of felled trees,
up the legion-rooted riverbank to this
unwilling masterwork of failed ambition:
a saltcellar, a wooden table, these

draw the landscape down to homely scale,
where table is a field upon which rises
the low barracks of a pigeon breast,
a rusty lake of wine, a silver palace

where the emperor drowns in salt and scans
the perfect ellipse of the emperor's sky.
How small it seems beneath this northern sky,
dark plums swelling in the indigo trees,

long pigs, snouts in the grass, groveling
for acorns. Only madness asks a man
to write business letters for a god.
High-heeled Octavian, whose lily palm

cupped the stink of blood, pricked Cicero dead—
severed hand silencing the Senate,
glazed eyes staring out of bodiless head.
The emperor digs our pasture in the thyme—

beyond the grave is grave beyond reach.
The gods pollute the altar of their speech.

Folly

Something of folly wipes the air
clean of its pretension, a woman
quilting madness into pattern, where

gold-threaded birds wing the compass rose
around a wounded tree the parliaments
of flowers choke. The mind's

many deliberations issue
from madness into love like muddy swans
breaching the bank for weeds their deep bills

cannot hold. They preen and sip
and otherwise complain their interest.
There is no love among them,

yet the madness clothed comes on again
and we call it love. But not ourselves,
though we word our declarations to our care.

I've watched three nights
the orb-weavers feast
on the window's steady light, funnel

down which throb the gold-eyed moths
they tangle in their webs and suck.
My face bares back at me

the black behind the glare, while breezes
mock sweet husks of insects spread
within the sticky circle of the dead.

Green Island

By runnels and sea-dipped clover, easing
water out of the headlands, the moon in daylight
scars the severed architecture back to grace.
God the competent, god the antique:

the green island arches
above water's shallow back
where brine shrimp scatter and the dark
unmannered boats troll. I measure the evil dates

spent staring the same blind channel
toward lumpish heaven. The water swelled
each evening in its grave surround,
the backlit island glowed and was gone.

And what was there, islanders?
Sand dyeing children's rags,
stolen keels athwart tattooed rocks,
beaches soaked with fisher's slaughter

where gray birds picked the wash for scraps.
What falls away each evening is not
kind authority: the cracked boats adrift,
abandoned swimmers lolling in the crawl,

no green ideal
toward whose curious carvings
one swimmer heads out with broken stroke,
a mote on the horizon, a silent O.

The Shootist

I do not think you know me.
I could be anyone
who comes from Atlanta or Athens,
Levittown or Babylon.

You probably know my girlfriend.
You've seen her on the screen
where light and shadow flicker
the Technicolor dreams.

She comes to me nightly—
Oh, yes she does—in sleep,
and says, "Oh, how I love you,
you're beautiful and deep,

and no one can ever hurt you
as long as I am near,
but it's morning, I have to be going—
you mustn't fear.

I'll come again this evening.
I'll come again for more.
I'll come in by the window
and leave by the back door."

She never stays for breakfast.
She never takes a meal.
The eggs look up like jaundice
by the talking cereal.

I have no mother or father,
no daughter and no son.
I have no past or future
but I have a little gun.

The handle's polished walnut,
the barrel's cold blue steel,
and six snug soldiers barrack
within the chambered wheel.

It has a shoulder holster
and a nasty trigger, too,
and six mad soldiers blossom
when I want them to.

You can see the holes in the ceiling
where I used to shoot at flies
and the holes in the television screen
where they tell lies,

because there won't be weather tomorrow
unless I want there to be.
There won't be any satellites
or any sea.

The sea's not blue in the darkness,
they say—but that can't be so.
What's blue is blue forever.
It's Death that won't let go.

Death's around every corner
though he can never be found.
That's why Death's so impressive—
he's the big man around.

I've seen them in the movies,
the killers and the killed.
They move like ballerinas.
They're elegant, they're skilled,

but they're only actors and actresses
and, then, aren't we all?—
waiting for the hour
we get the agent's call

and step out by the footlights
and bow to that applause
more delicious than truth or beauty
and louder than laws.

My girl never stays till daylight.
She lives in secrecy,
meeting I-don't-know-who, doing I-don't-know-what.
I want her to notice me

not just in the dark of the bedroom
where there's no light but the moon.
The moon is mad and lonely,
but he sings in tune,

singing, "Where are all the lovers
from all years past?
Death and sleep sleep together
but love never lasts.

I remember Eden and Athens,
Paradise and Babylon.
Love would last forever
if you had a little gun.

Show your lover you love her.
Show her that you know
Death and sleep lie together.
She'll never let you go."

I'm in a hotel waiting,
watching a man on t.v.
I can see him on three channels
but he can't see me.

Tomorrow I'll take a stroll
down by his hotel
where he'll be talking and talking
like a guy with a car to sell.

I'll wait for him on the corner.
I'll wait till he walks by,
where I can see in his empty eyes
the empty sky.

I have no mother or father,
no daughter and no son,
no past and no future,
but I have a little gun.

The King of Black Pudding

In the dusty and blood-soaked shop
he could not reason the declining regard
for the blood sausage and Barnsley chop—

hacked from Southdown sheep,
two chops per sheep, the Barnsley chops
the Prince of Wales could not complete

three years before his abdication.
Albert Hirst did not complain.
A purveyor of pudding must know his station,

but no matrix or linear algebra
could calculate a value for
the caviar of the North, curse of anaemia.

Each morning he swallowed a slice
or two, to qualify his ware.
Though his manner was very precise,

on his ribs reposed a weight
one likes to see on a butcher
or a pig at the slaughterer's gate.

The pigs despite their brooding
cannot serve as pallbearers
for the king of black pudding.

Flour Mites as Moral Beings

Born to a desert we die in bread,
and if the repetition of our labors
cannot be approved, who, discovering

our secretive gorging, our clumsy
mating in a bed of sand, can condemn
a habitat we cannot alter, knowing

no intimate prospect but whiteness?
Monstrous to others,
we have come to prefer our minute

diffidence, each a stranger to his parents
as to his children. Who can say
equality has not given us

an appreciation of loneliness?
All our languages are conjugated in silence,
our etiquette colored by modesty,

our sex legislated by need, never desire.
Can we be condemned because
our philosophers have fouled themselves

with the available, our engineers
narrowed their figures toward
Those-Who-Determine? We accept

the sufficient ignorance of our situation.
We are, at least, masters of our dry economy,
not parasites of flesh—and so not

religious—nor like our cousins ruthless
cannibals, uncivilized though hugely beautiful
with intricate rites and dew-laden nets.

This Island

Strata's dip and strike, reason's rippled sea,
nor any flooded scar prepares
the wreckage of this wandering plain.
Beaches rattle the rusting chain and open

the coiled ammonite, but undergrowth
cannot profane the cottage
fouled by fire, nor the withered apple sprout
palatable leaves. Dingy sheep

the black dogs worry
bleat into their painted wool
while sharp beaks rustle through heather
to hollow eggs. How is their spotted color

the eyes' domain? The keeper
rattles to his boss, and four or five
vacation houses flame the eastern sky,
toys taken for tinder.

Down the cobbled walk
a body crouches bleeding from its knees.
A hooded man tenders his pistol.
Dry streambeds fill with startled flocks.

Whatever You Say Say Nothing

This morning light erasing the night damages
uncolors what would ease a wakefulness:
scored like a skull, our one star rages

over the plain hulls of the hills.
What surveying snail discovers
or worm tempted forth by dew

is hostility undergrowth bears
scars of the visible. Domestic, domestic,
cry the birds tangled in vines.

Muck the Roman road burrows in
accepts the horse's print; its calks argue
against a history in whose airy parlor

larval brick or stone emerges,
patient for the slow shudder of metamorphosis.
Night seas slide without value,

but here shadows heal unkempt fissures,
no inscription marring withered leaf.
Though orders of silence rule

fish corrupted on the shore,
talkative sailors still turn their seines:
to see is a violent naming.

The nautical farmer, weaned from wrecks,
sails out into his wheat, tacking
his unseasoned harvester

past the ruined badger in its hole.
Artificial structures of the eye
bend a natural landscape back: I am not

immune to the rising of the horned moon,
fierce as a samurai helmet,
the moon that polishes slate hours

until starched men on the line,
torsos separated from their legs,
shine in salt light, until the evening bed

where you clothe your genitals in silk
shines like a coffin. Salt's ceremonies of regard
apply to wounds no tool of nature makes.

The island men have in their heads
no compass or thermometer, know only
a feathered clockwork on its post,

errant starling swiveling on its branch,
whose troubled feathers crawl with green-black light.
The mute lie murdered in complicity.

Our Life Thus Far

On heated planets the heated inhabitants
make little of our season;
lives partial to loss if not leisure
find real pain an intransigent reason.

Dead mallard iridescent in green river.
Sparrows mating on hard clay.
Even into science comes a light
colder than spring. In cloisonné,

for example, the local chapel's stained glass
discolors equally the sinner and shaved,
but sex is no dispassionate litmus
for the honest among the depraved.

You and I look out different windows
as if one darkens less than others—
of the passing young girls in flame skirts
some are ignorant enough, already, to be mothers.

L'Histoire d'Angleterre

I

The old dactyls gather along raked sand,
feathers of birds scattered in the trash.
To the tourist, a modeled field, garden
not of pallid gods but geese; to the farmer,
eruptive sore. The love of what it leaves behind.

A sour light inoculates from war the dens
and vengeful arias riddling the fens,

acidic texture rusting trees to men,

bog oak, becket, the dancing grain.

Consumptive, digestion cannot ignore
what spade and brush will find:
medicine of chariots, bronze armors
hollow as examination mirrors,
coiled lieutenants gasping in the tar.

II

Scarecrow gripping torn plastic bag

flatters the field his brothers cannot reach:
cold fury of appetite. Age preserve
the ruined face that reamed Scottish stock: leached
by unrepentant shores on which they beached.

The master eats again the bloody caul,
pencil cancels what pen inscribes.

Sailor's deadeyes tighten before squall,
upon the wind a tourniquet. Preach tartan
to the hanged man, wanderings of tribe
unevenly sexed. Minister emergency: exit text.

A little entertainment the common lot
of all who venture upon foreign airs:
flotsam not jetsam clusters the strand.

III

Tongueless warriors beg from camp to camp.
Caulescent history nipped at ground,

thorn not in briars but books:
the brick wall undulating toward
colonial proprieties, umbrellas guarding
ladies from the blacks, the sun.

Petrol tanker wired to border checkpoint,
broken glass in milk, mined hedge
improvise where older law prevails:
Catholic marries bullets from Catholic guns.

Local sun rises over veldt and heath,
though border insists what farmer describes.
The open mouths dispute charges

to the death the poor insist on, bribes.